INTERNET ISSUES

SHOPPING

BY

SHALINI VALLEPUR

BookLife PUBLISHING

©2022
BookLife Publishing Ltd.
King's Lynn, Norfolk
PE30 4LS, UK

All rights reserved.
Printed in Poland.

A catalogue record for
this book is available from
the British Library.

ISBN: 978-1-80155-187-8

Written by:
Shalini Vallepur

Edited by:
John Wood

Designed by:
Danielle Rippengill

IMAGE CREDITS

All images are courtesy of Shutterstock.com, unless otherwise specified. With thanks to Getty Images, Thinkstock Photo and iStockphoto. Front Cover – Bloomicon, Alex Gontar, George Rudy, New Africa, Twin Design. Images used on every page – Bloomicon, Alex Gontar. 2 – Bloomicon. 4–5 – Aquarius Studio, George Rudy, Monkey Business Images. 6–7 – Andrey_Popov, aslysun, Monkey Business Images. 8–9 – Dragon Images, LightField Studios, McLittle Stock, Mr_Mrs_Marcha, Worawee Meepian. 10–11 – Kaspars Grinvalds, Rawpixel.com, Tomek_Pa. 12–13 – EugeneEdge, Rawpixel.com, Sam72. 14–15 – Andrew Rybalko, BoxerX, SynthEx. 16–17 – McLittle Stock, Sam72, solarseven. 18–19 – fizkes, New Afric, _shutte. 20–21 – fizkes, Iurii Stepanov, Rawpixel.com. 22–23 – Dragon Images, Sarawut Chainawara.

CONTENTS

WORDS THAT LOOK LIKE this CAN BE FOUND IN THE GLOSSARY ON PAGE 24.

THE INTERNET

Have you ever been on the internet? The internet is something we use to connect computers, smartphones and tablets around the world.

+1

People all over the world use the internet every day. The internet can be used for work, to learn, to buy things and to talk to other people.

SHOPPING ON ⊗ THE INTERNET

ONLINE SHOPPING

Many grown-ups use the internet to buy things. This is called online shopping. Online shopping lets people buy things without going out to the shop.

SHOPPING

ONLINE MEANS ON THE INTERNET.

6

Things that are bought online need to be paid for with money, just like when things are bought in a shop.

Some shops have their own **websites** and **apps**. You can buy what you need and it gets sent straight to your house.

£

YOU CAN BUY FOOD FROM SUPERMARKETS OR FROM SUPERMARKET WEBSITES.

Some websites allow many people and shops to sell things. These are called e-commerce websites.

INFORMATION

Online shops and websites usually need your personal information. You may have to use an **email address** to make an **account** with a username and password.

EMAIL ADDRESS

USERNAME

PASSWORD

BANK DETAILS

WHERE YOU LIVE

NEVER SHARE YOUR PERSONAL INFORMATION ONLINE OR WITH PEOPLE YOU DO NOT KNOW.

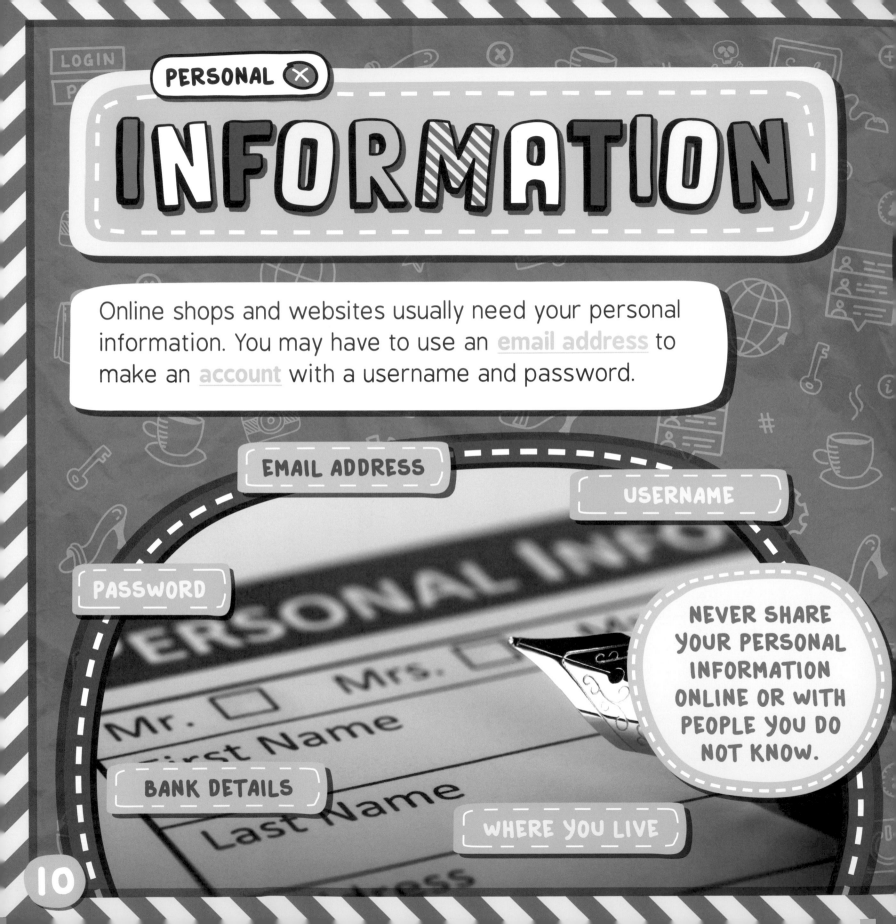

Mr.

Mrs.

First Name

Last Name

A bank account is where grown-ups keep their money safe. A shopping website usually needs a person's bank details to pay for the things they want to buy.

SCAMS

Scams are when a person or a website lies to you or tricks you into doing something. They may try to trick people into sharing their personal information and bank details.

If a person gets scammed, their personal information could be stolen. This information could be used to steal their money.

SPOTTING ⊗ SCAMS

SCAM ALERT!
with caution

It is important to know how to spot an online shopping scam. Checking the **URL** of a website is a good place to start.

NOT SECURE   HTTP://WWW.BUYCLOTHES.SHOP.GIVE-MONEY.CO.UK/

SCAM WEBSITES MAY NOT HAVE A PADLOCK SYMBOL.

THE URL OF A SCAM WEBSITE OFTEN STARTS WITH 'HTTP' INSTEAD OF 'HTTPS'.

!CLICK HERE TO WIN!

TOTAL SCAM! ITEM NEVER SHOWED UP!

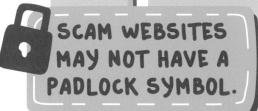

THERE MAY BE LOTS OF POP-UP advertisements.

SCAM WEBSITES MAY HAVE BAD reviews.

POP-UPS

Pop-ups are advertisements that can suddenly appear on the screen. They can be hard to avoid and you might click on one accidentally.

SOME POP-UPS MAY EVEN GIVE YOUR **device** A **virus**.

MALWARE

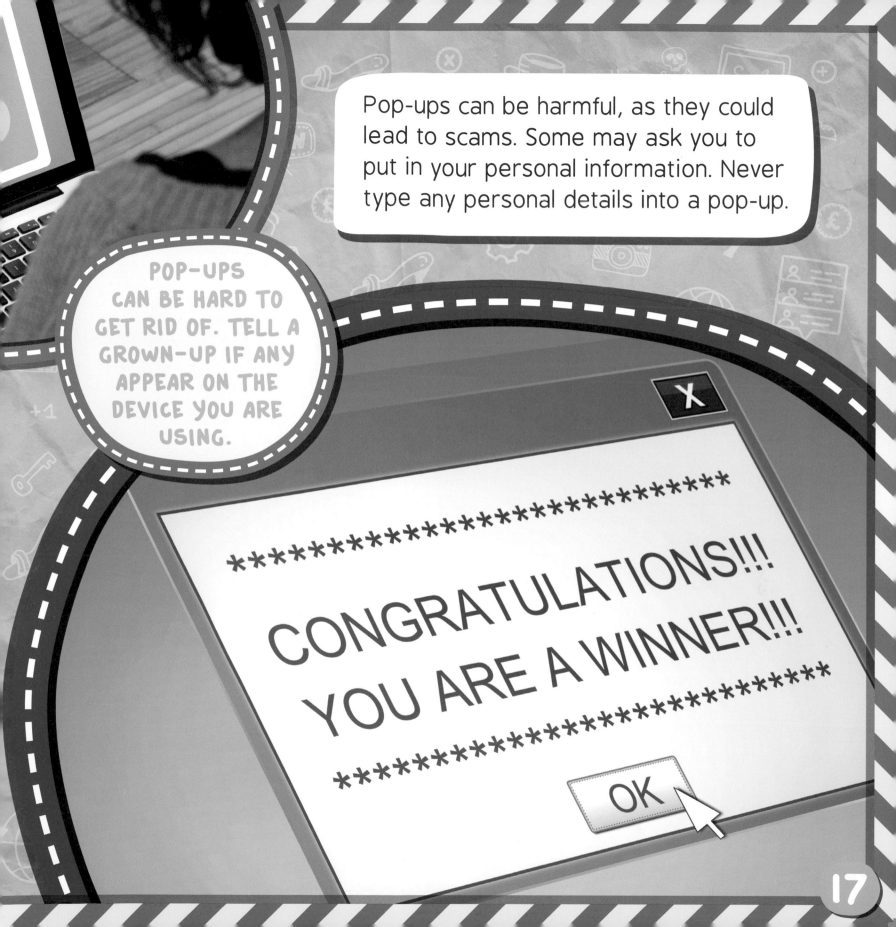

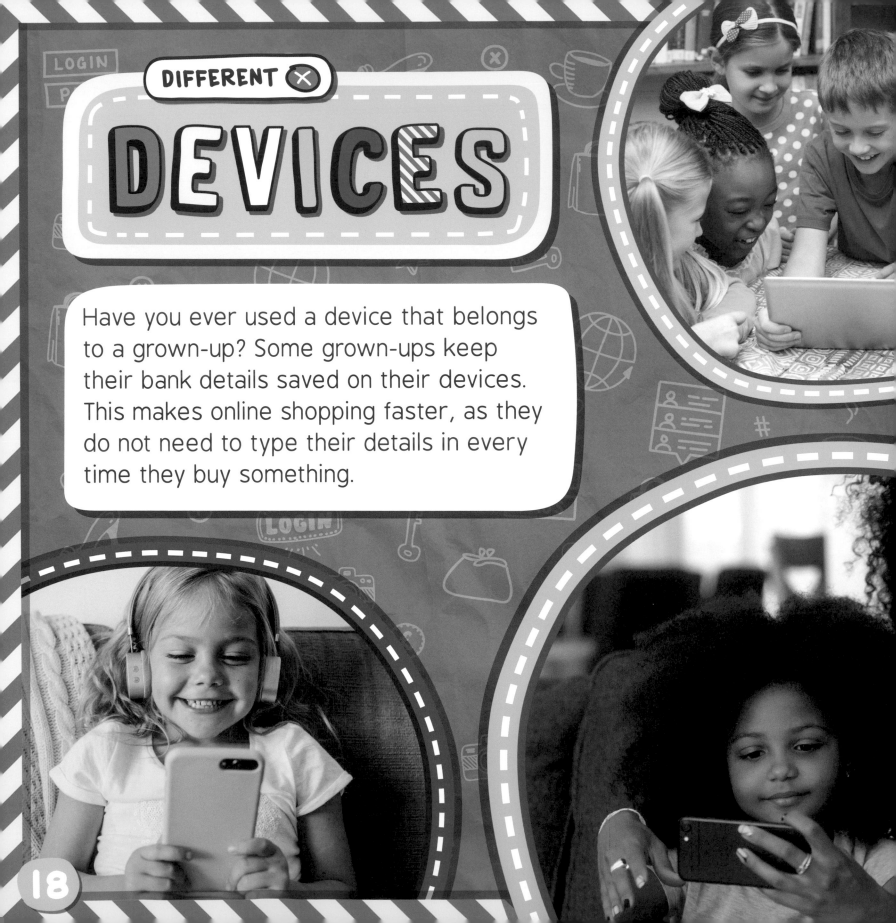

DIFFERENT ⊗

DEVICES

Have you ever used a device that belongs to a grown-up? Some grown-ups keep their bank details saved on their devices. This makes online shopping faster, as they do not need to type their details in every time they buy something.

IF YOU BUY SOMETHING ACCIDENTALLY, DO NOT PANIC — TELL THE GROWN-UP STRAIGHT AWAY.

When using somebody else's device, it is important to make sure you do not accidentally buy something online. It can be easy to buy lots of things when you do not mean to.

SAFE AND ⊗ SECURE

ANTI VIRUS

QUICK SCAN
SCANNING...

C:\RawPixel\Pixel.NET\Framework\v6.03.072\web

2855 files

14 minutes, 22 seconds left.

STOP   PAUSE   RESUME

please wait...
your computer is scanning

UPDATE

Online shopping is useful for many people, but it is important to look out for scams, pop-ups and viruses. Most devices can have security programs added to them.

ce_validate(self, cr, uid, ids, context=
f.generate_ebInterface(cr, uid, ids, context=
return super(account_invoices,self).invoice_validate(
invoice_validate

ff generate ebInter
for invoice in s
template chi = self.pool.
if not template_ids :

**WARNING!
VIRUS DETECTED!**

(_("Customization Error !")
(_("No Template "%s" defined")

Security programs can help stop scams and pop-ups from harming devices. Talk to a grown-up or ask them to show you how to make sure a device has security settings on.

21

NEED TO KNOW

Now you know some of the ways of shopping online, and some of the dangers, too. Let's go over some of the things we have learnt.

POP-UPS CAN LEAD TO SCAMS OR VIRUSES.

SECURITY PROGRAMS CAN KEEP OUR DEVICES SAFE.

A SAFE URL STARTS WITH 'HTTPS' AND A PADLOCK SYMBOL.

GLOSSARY

ACCOUNT	part of a website or game that stores information about you that is used to get onto some parts of the internet
ADVERTISEMENTS	posters, videos or pictures that tell people about things that are for sale
APPS	programs that work on mobile devices such as smartphones or tablets
DEVICE	an electronic machine that is made for a particular purpose, such as a smartphone, tablet, games console or computer
EMAIL ADDRESS	a combination of letters, numbers and symbols that only you have which are linked to an email account where people can send messages called emails to
REVIEWS	comments left about a product, service or experience that talk about whether it is good or not
URL	the address for a webpage
VIRUS	a piece of code that can cause harm to a device and the programs on it
WEBSITES	places on the internet that are usually made up of several webpages

INDEX